Gray Streak

a poetry collection

Tyler G. Freitas

insensate publication

Sweet Darkness

When your eyes are tired
the world is tired also.

When your vision has gone,
no part of the world can find you.

Time to go into the dark
where the night has eyes
to recognize its own.

There you can be sure
you are not beyond love.

The dark will be your home
tonight.

The night will give you a horizon
further than you can see.

You must learn one thing.
The world was made to be free in.

Give up all the other worlds
except the one to which you belong.

Sometimes it takes darkness and the sweet
confinement of your aloneness
to learn

anything or anyone
that does not bring you alive

is too small for you.

—David Whyte

Table of Contents

For Leo.

Acknowledgements

This collection would not have come to light without the feedback and support from my parents; my wife, Ariel; my friends, J.D. Oyan, Patrick Lahey, and P. Brady; and my mentor, Mark Cotta Vaz.

Thank you,

Tyler G. Freitas

Also by Tyler G. Freitas

Flow Commotion

Superlova

You were a guiding light
leading the way
You were burning bright
til your dying day

Withholding

When I look in the carts of fellow
grocery shoppers, I want to yell,
"Put the Oreos back,
break the Kit-Kats,
throw the junk in the trash!
Buy fresh, bright juicy produce:
Oranges that burst to the bite,
apples for warm cider at night, and
leafy greens that are dark and deep!"

Untethering

To acknowledge our existence, is to suffer:
a dialectic between "I" and the universe.
Cut the thread—no more tangles and tethers.

Ripples

There is no sound in space
Waves of light greet the eye
Smile, and embrace the silence.

insensate

If you feel grounded – grow wings
If you feel stupid – read a book
If you feel tired – rest
If you feel nothing –

Walden Pond

Pines and maples dampen the sound
    of passing cars.
Plump, white women swing with bright
floaties
    attached to their hips.
Are there fish beneath the surface?
Is the pond a portal to an alternate reality?
If I squint my eyes, will I see Emerson and
    Thoreau staring back at me?
If I set my ear against Monet's paintings
    in the Museum of Fine Art,
Will I hear the birds flying outside the frame?

Tavern Signs

The Harvard Library is closed to the public—literacy was low in Boston.

Corpus

Gather all of the art and literature
Burn it.
Build a new, beautiful body.

Flock Coat

I bought a gray Patagonia quarter-zip
to blend in with the white sheeple.

Stay Inside

Northern California is on fire again:
Smoke-filled skies in September,
The aftermath of a tiny ember
Flaming acres that never end –
Incinerating families and friends.

Crunch

My ego is crumbling like a curled leaf
    at the end of Fall,
stomped into the ground,
    and scattered about the field
where we used to play.

Leo

I haven't even met you,
    but I already let you go.
Filling every room with warmth,
    even when it snows.

Golf

Swing smoothly through the ball.
Do not look up too soon.
Twist the hips, the hands will follow.
Let the club do the work.

Idealism

Renewable energy firms use fossil fuels
to meet at offices in SF with food and booze,
complaining about crumbling infrastructure—
yet they can't swing a hammer
to save their lives.

Bruised Ego

It took decades of degradation
to foment the discontent that
fertilized the grounds for bigoted
seeds to grow into a tree of hate—
turning the joys of life into bitter fruit.

Unaccountable

Hosting a Bad Poetry Contest
is a great way to degrade
an art form, and lower expectations.
No need to justify crimes with explanations.
Religious wars raging in the Middle East
don't concern citizens in my nation:
A couple weeks pass, then we're on vacation.

Table Scraps

I've played enough poker to notice
a crack in a laugh or smile;
some people can conceal it for a while,
but time blows the sand off the glass
and reveals what lies beneath:
Their insecurities and traumatic past—
I used to be kind—but kept eating last.

Doom & Gloom

Californians forgot US history—
fixated on the latest murder mystery
and twinkling technological gadgets—
breeding anxiety like rabbits.

Passing the Torch

My baby grows
before the first flakes of snow
fall in mid-November.

Four more months until his cries
arrive at our front door,
shaking the window panes—
and plenty of dirty shirt stains.

Obsolescence

A samurai with the sharpest sword
and sound strategy,
falls to the sniper hiding in the hills.

The Kids Aren't Alright

Drone drops bombs on babies—
the teenage pilot sets the controls aside,
opens a soda, and scrolls through socials.

Linguistic Trickery

Labels diminish entities:
      people, places, flavors—
obscuring the totality and unity
      of our shared existence.

Words are far too bountiful to be
      bandied about by idle brains;
Truth won't be revealed by radicals,
      Your utopia is less than ideal.

Born in the Bay

The Bay Area is an amazing place,
because of the diversity.
To be fearful of mentioning the
color of our citizens' skin
would run the risk of neglecting
our cultural diversity.

We must acknowledge our judgements,
and inculcate kindness.
We cannot put people on pedestals,
when wants change like the wind.

Status Quo

Capitalism and the exchange of goods
     creates an economy.
Everyone involved complicitly accepts
     the commodities and infrastructure.
A switch for lights; a tap for water;
     ordering food from our cell phones.

We will fight and die to maintain
     the status quo.
Everyone is an adversary,
     turning neighbors into foes.

Christmas Past

String lights on houses in early December
The days grow colder, an ax chops timber
The family is shrinking, tough to remember
Smiles on faces, and warmth from embers.

Fanatics

Christmas trees are missing branches,
War is destroying farms and ranches;
Religious differences and sacred sites—
Corrupting minds turn wrongs to rights.

Determined

Determined by Robert Sapolsky

You are at the mercy of your biology
 and environment.
The path forward was predetermined
 before you were born:
Every single decision—from beliefs
 to clothes worn.

We are all victims of cosmological
 consequences:
Struggling and scrapping for comfort
 and contentment.

Blind Faith

A blind man walked off the cement path
      alongside a diner, into a bush.
A blind, elderly woman collided with
      an orange cone set out on the street.
They both grasped at their obstruction,
      then continued their journey;
assured and unafraid of other obstacles
      that will impede their progress.

Renee

The eccentric, spinster owner
built a book barricade to obstruct
the suffering souls on B Street.

Ariel

She's cleaning every corner and crevice
Assembling a crib and folding clothes
Arranging diapers and blankets;
Radiating more light than the sun.

Winter Mourning

It's the sheet of ice on your car's window
the white cloud rising from warm breath
the dark puddle splashing onto the sidewalk
the drop of dew that contains multitudes—
eternally dripping into a pool of solitude.

Pre-memory

In the beginning, our parents' fingers
were thick like an oak tree branch;
bareskin was cold and uncomfortable,
and we didn't have control of our bodies.
Our caregivers tried to shield us
from the drug-filled streets and buses,
afraid that the darkness would consume our
sanity, and hope for humanity.

Dogs in the Woods

Dogs stare at
humans shitting
on toilets
with the utmost envy.

An Easy Mile

Sipping five dollar coffee
from unknown origins and
stepping over homeless people,
with expensive shoes
that tap along the sidewalk;
unyielding and indifferent.

Evicted: Part I

Evicted by Matthew Desmond

If you are a poor, black single mother
in the USA—you are a burden:
landlords will reject you—
or if they accept you, they neglect you;
broken window, clogged drain, leaky roof.
Government agencies will deny benefits;
then they'll turn off the gas
in the middle of a white, winter night, and
movers will toss belongings to the curb,
or into an unaffordable storage unit.
Family and friends will turn away in shame.

Who are we to blame?

Starving kids eat lead paint and go insane.

Evicted: Part II

Evicted by Matthew Desmond

Men are losing their legs because
they don't have medical benefits
to treat a routine wound.
Laborers tweak their backs, bones crack,
so they swallow a handful of opioids:
until every shred of dignity is destroyed.
Is the texture of rock bottom the same?
After all hope has gone down the drain;
mental fog clouds and darkens the brain.
Is the texture of suffering the same?

Evicted: Part III

Evicted by Matthew Desmond

It's easy to profit off of the poor—
turn an angel into a whore;
turning tricks in the morning for more
money, to buy food and supplies,
lying to your kid about the black eye
bullets flying outside . . . teen dies.
How many parents have to cry
before hearts swell, and leaders rise?

Quiet and White

Inspired by Matthew Desmond's *Poverty, By America*

Poverty in the USA is the greatest trap.
Affluent individuals influence elections
to hoard wealth, then denounce the poor:
lazy bums, slackers, and low lifes.
Eventually, all strata of society agrees—
believing an easy lie to keep our
neighborhoods quiet and white.

Brian

is selling newspapers at the top
of Embarcadero BART's stairs for
$2 a piece, to buy new teeth.
It took him 30 days to hitchhike
from Colorado. Now, the City
pays for him to stay in a hotel;
where he composes love poems
for the women that got away.

The Poverty Plague

Inspired by Matthew Desmond's *Poverty, By America*

It is not a matter of resources.
We are the wealthiest nation,
but we allow elites to control rations
and deny the poor a chance for recourse.
Media would have us believe that poverty
is a disease, with no cure or remedy—
yet the expense of sick, uneducated people
outweighs the cost of proactive investment.

Packaging

Baby products have too much packaging;
my recycling bin is bulging at the brim—
most of the materials are meant for the trash,
but the trash was full the night before last.

Free Market

Since when did microplastics
and pesticides cause harm?
If a good is elastic,
why sound the alarm?

Slovenly Spectators

Sports are billion dollar businesses.
Athletes train for decades to compete—
while the fans get fat, and swollen feet.

Expectations

Trust is tenuous when no one knows
their neighbors, and what they believe—
myriad versions of the American Dream—
streets are empty, except for crows.

Egotist

Every artist is arrogant enough
to believe in the import of their creations:
studying forms, from smooth to rough—
constantly seeking thrills and elations.

Dunce

Inspired by John Kennedy Toole's *A Confederacy of Dunces*

Ignatius Reilly is a wily one,
a twentieth century Don Quixote
a flatulent flabbergaster
an intellectual deviant
a leech and pestilence upon society;
accumulating scraps of writing,
alongside discarded food wrappers;
belittling and overworking his mom.
Hubris and apathy are a dangerous mix;
so addictive, that even drugs cannot fix.

Freed..

It is uncomfortable
to believe that life is
predetermined.
Biology is heavily influenced
by environmental factors—
who am I to believe in
controlling my actions?

You Suffer, We Suffer

"It is no measure of health to be well adjusted to a profoundly sick society." —Jiddu Krishnamurti

We're so quick to label people—
put them in boxes and bury them
in the back of our minds; praying
that they don't rise from graves,
depraved, from our forsaking—
preventing an awakening
to our collective existence.

Doorbell Camera

Nature is constantly encroaching:
biological hordes approaching;
bacteria, fungi, predators—
keep surfaces clean,
and lock your doors.

Yuppie Trap

$15 for a cappuccino and matcha
white yuppies walking by—gotcha!

Now You Know

Chinese New Year
is now
Lunar New Year—
pass it along.

Built Upon Bones

Four Chinese immigrants were blown up
in the building of Lake Chabot.
Were their corpses recovered and buried,
or were they left at the site where dynamite
exploded and caved in the excavated walls;
encased beneath the 135-foot concrete dam?

Look Up and Act

People read and stare at
their phones on BART,
because they're too afraid
to stare at other passengers;
especially the drug-addled
and destitute people.
Some are too far gone,
beyond the reach of rehabilitation,
and that is okay. We can still help
the poor and hungry today,
and reverse the trend.

Environments will heal
when given time—as long as
invasive species are managed.

Providing solutions and taking
action is laborious, but apathy
and inaction are not viable options.

Master List

I made a list
to keep track of
all my lists,
but I tossed it
while cleaning.

Segregated

I thought I understood the perspective of social liberals and progressives, but now it seems like they are more concerned about craft beer, single-origin coffee, thrifted clothes.

For the Gram

Whole lives are wasted, expending energy
to show others how great things appear—
while the kids run wild, pets are ignored,
and the leaky roof creates colonies of mold.

Code Violation

I approach poetry like a contractor:
rising before the sun, dressing
in the dark, massaging my sore neck,
and bodily aches—consuming coffee.

Books serve as my building guides;
pen and paper are my only tools.

Sometimes the form and foundation
are strong, and the words string together
to form a beautiful, seamless tapestry—
but other days, the ending is out of place,
and the rhythm is shaky—sending the edifice
        sideways,
                crushing innocent readers;
who were searching for a beam of light.

Instead, they are covered in ash and dust.

Unstoppable

I want my son to be faster,
stronger, kinder, and wiser;
the captain of his destiny,
master of body and mind –
free of the anxieties
and expectations that
cloud, haunt, and confuse.

Family

The people that you love most—
after they have moved on.

Deep Sleep

Another week of rain and wind
lashing at my bedroom window—
while I rest on my Purple mattress,
snug and warm by my wife's side—
beyond the ego, slipping into slumber,
undisturbed by lightning and thunder.

The Offering

Rest gently baby
Grab a handful of stardust
Sprinkle it about.

Adopted

Abandoned at birth by parents
who weren't prepared to bear
the burden of raising a child.
Constantly scanning strangers
on the street for acceptance.

Neglect

Staring through the window of your
parent's car, looking for approval
on the side of an empty freeway,
patiently waiting to play.

Dream Chasing

Wandering through a field of flowers,
while opportunities pass like ants
trailing to and from their nest—
we keep running, but don't get far.

Teadious

Teacup at the table's edge.
Fists slam the surface
sending it over,
into the void—
s h a t t e r i n g
into a million shards.
I want to piece it back together,
but she told me not to bother.

Self Preservation

In general, honesty is the best policy—
unless a woman asks you how she looks.

Spare the Children

Children learn quickly
because we don't shame them
for their ignorance.

Arrival

His head is crowning.
An eternity passes
between contractions.
The world stands still—
until it hears him cry.

Lucecito

All of my pains and trials feel
insignificant when face-to-face
with my laboring wife:
bent over in anguish;
breathing and pushing
to bring new life to the light.

Moral Math

Do not swim in Lake Chabot,
that's where the algae grows.
The Bay and California shores
are filled with trash and more.
We could've built clean and strong,
but moral costs broke the budget.

"Other" Half

When people sneer at multiracial couples,
do they see the smiles on their faces;
the warmth in their laughter, or the
harmony of two hands held together:
A bond that grows stronger in the face
of abuse and bigotry—past and future.

Phantoms in the Factory

I would shake the hand of the child
who stitched my shirt—if they hadn't
lost it to the factory machine.

Insatiable

83

I really worked up an appetite while
reading about the Dutch Hunger Winter.

Equalizer

Regardless of your caste—
explosive baby shit on your shirt
will make you untouchable.

Eat, Sleep, Shit, Repeat

Sleeping in one hour stints at night
dims and drains the daylight;
causing nerves to twist and fray,
and dark thoughts that we dare not say.

Cold Hands

Having a baby is a beautiful thing—
but the passionless congratulations; and
condescending comments from hospital staff
are colder than the touch of a latexed hand
during a routine genital examination.

Saul's Deli

87

Take a bite of the Pastrami Ruskie;
schmear apple sauce and crema on the latke;
and sip the hot toddy on a cool morning.
Now, how could anyone hate the Jews?

Acculturation

88

If the South rises again, and loses,
we should force them to speak Spanish.

Necesita Jardineros

The biggest bigots could greatly
benefit from some latino landscaping.

A Balanced Beverage

I like my water with
a good deal of PFAS
plenty of phthalates
heaps of fluoride
a sprinkle of lead
a twist of non-organic,
pesticide orange peel.

A Delicious Plan

91

I drafted a daily dietary plan for my
morbidly obese family member,
which took up several pages.
They said it tasted a bit bland.

I was going to . . .

Instead of scrolling on social media,
I could start a garden in my backyard;
volunteer at a homeless shelter;
read a book to my newborn child . . .

Wow, this dog sure knows how to dance!

Micro Aggression

We should shrink
the stigma of
tiny penises—
there's a palpable
lack of pleasure.

Vanilla Fortune Cookie

Appropriating cultures is bad,
but honoring them is good—
so I eat with chopsticks and a fork,
because that is the Middle Way.

Content

I thought new clothes,
fast cars, and stiff drinks
would make me happy,
but the highs were fleeting—
and the lows kept sinking;
nothing could fill the void.

Now,

I want just enough rain
to keep the hills green;
just enough food
to feel satiated;
and just enough life,
to die satisfied.

Mas Amor

It's better
to fall
in love—
than rise
in hatred.

Bravery

97

We are always minutes away
from a thermonuclear winter.
A few brave people have prevented
mutually assured destruction—
while the masses bicker about politics.

Only the Great Survive

All mindless labor will be automated away—
only the intelligent and skilled will remain:
Strive for greatness, or get in line for UBI.

Lab Rats

Science smites magic and mythology;
religion recedes where rationalism rises,
there won't be decisions or surprises
when governments program our biology.

Docility

Give us your guns.
We'll pay your bills.
Do not try to run.
Keep taking your pills.

Outbreak

Biology cannot be contained indefinitely; eventually, a specimen will break free and wreak havoc on our vulnerabilities.

Exposed

Some poets bare their souls:
standing naked on the page
for everyone to see—
all of their deformities;
bald spots and sagging skin.
Hiding from the cries and lies
of several passersby in July.

Dear Francium

If atoms were slightly less stable,
my hopes and worries would explode.

Cute and Stinky

My son makes the cutest faces,
and squirms like a worm—
bringing joy to my wife and I—
before filling his diaper with waste.

Double-dealing

We give aid and arms to Ukraine—
while continuing to buy Russian oil.

All for One

Communism seems great—
until you study twentieth century
Chinese and Russian History.

Hunger Thoughts

Writing while hungry
keeps the mind lean.

Grounded

When the plane takes off,
and the wheels leave the ground:
I feel the limitless potential of mankind—
but one stray seagull could humble us all.

Plant Killers

109

Before criticizing carnivores,
rip a plant from the ground;
watch the leaves wilt
and the roots wither.

Gray Streak

Without loved ones,
victories are vacuous,
losses loom large,
and the days coalesce:

like smearing charcoal lines,
leaving a light gray streak
that reminds us what remains,
when life loses all its color.

Locus of Control

A newborn can see
8 to 15 inches;
anything further
is out of focus—
and irrelevant.

Signaling

Bees dance to disseminate information
about the location and quality of pollen.
Ants leave a trail of pheromones
for foraging comrades to follow.
Humans take to the street in cities
to fight for their personal freedoms.

Shared Interests

Mephisto and religious leaders
are both adept at using fear,
to frighten people into believing;
and followers sacrifice their lives,
hoping to attain the greatest glory.

Essential Elements

A pearl cannot form
without the first grit of sand.

Max Occupancy

I run naked
through the rain—
shouting inane,
insane things—
to keep the
crazies away.

No Ayuda Aqui

The California State Disability Office
    is a sordid establishment.
Roughly 50% of the applicants
    are Spanish speakers,
but the office workers no hablan,
    so everyone is annoyed.

Protecting our Pride

We're supposed to believe that
the Egyptians fought with swords,
yet possessed a novel technology
to build the pyramids, which align
with the star in our solar system.

Sports > Art

Tens of thousands of people
gather in a stadium to watch
a few dozen men put a ball
through a round, red hoop—
while most artists struggle
to put food on their table.

Alcoholism

The river flowed innocently at first,
before colliding with jagged rocks,
then roaring, foaming white rapids,
which ruptured relational rafts.
Some occupants made it ashore—
others drowned on the river's floor.

Crowing Around

Crows caw and dance
in the oak tree
behind my house;
gossiping about
the neighborhood, and
flaunting their feathers.

Always Alone

Dangling dreams and desires
like new shoes on a power line,
to distract and mislead the mind
away from the beauty of solitude.

First Frost

The student bows deeply,
then lunges forth with sword—

the master parries and ripostes,

a scream startles the bunny
living under a dying wisteria—
a drop of blood on the window,
whitened from the first frost.

The Boobie Brawler

Fear the ferocity
of a hungry newbie:
bobbing and weaving
biting and clawing
an innocent boobie.

Growing Soft

Most house plants
wouldn't last a day
in these streets.

Shelved

Who do you think you are
riding in his car?
You told me we'd go far—
now, I'm a fallen star.

I was staring in the mirror;
trying to find myself.
I was searching for truth
Now, I'm stuck on a shelf.

We used to hold hands,
but now I'm a hassle,
so I built you a castle
that sank in the sand.

Pessoas

I would pay anything
to know Fernando Pessoa—
I'm sure he would, too.

Unperturbed

If I let every comment
cause consternation,
I'd be curled in a ball
in the corner of my closet.

Anxious

Endings are assured,
but the anticipation
of starting fresh
freezes the fingers.